My friend Jake has Autism

Christine Draper

This is my friend Jake. I love playing with Jake. We run around and have fun. Jake can climb very high on the playground equipment.

I have fun talking to Jake. He has told me he has something called autism. That means he is autistic. I said that it is cool to have an autistic friend.

Jake is very bright. He is really good at math, much better than me. Jake said that people with autism range in their ability at school from very bright like him, to others who struggle and go to special schools. I said that I am glad that he is clever because he can help me.

2+4=6
5+3=8

Jake is constantly fiddling. The teacher sometimes gives him something to fiddle with. He says that it helps him to concentrate better. Even though he looks like he isn't paying attention, he really can remember things better if he is fiddling.

I went to a fair with Jake once. It was very noisy, with lots of lights. To me, it looked really exciting, but Jake hated it. Later, I asked him why. He said that it was because, being autistic, he has a problem with something called sensory processing.

I didn't know what that meant. He told me that it means that someone is affected by sights, sounds, touch or taste differently to other people. In some people, it means that they seek out particular senses and for other people, they avoid them. He said that, for him, it is a mixture of both.

Sometimes sounds or sights bother him much more than me. That is because he can't filter them out like I can. One day in art class, the tap in the room was dripping. I stopped noticing it after a while, but Jake found it really difficult to deal with because, to him, it sounded much louder than I heard it.

I can remember, when he was younger, he loved superheroes. He had this superman costume and would ask to put it on. However, as soon as it was on, he would be asking to take it off because he couldn't stand the feel of it. I asked if this is what he meant. "Yeah," he said.

He told me that for some people, sensory issues affect just one sense. For other people, it can affect more than one. He said, for him, it also affected taste. I laughed, remembering him coming to my house for dinner and he ate the spaghetti but with no sauce. His mom was really embarrassed, but my mom said that it was OK, as we are all different with different tastes.

Jake has a particular interest in steam trains. So, he is always talking about what he knows and even the differences between the different engines. It gets really annoying sometimes. Mom told me that sometimes autistic people develop a particular interest in something. Now, I sometimes say, "Jake, can we please talk about something else?" He will normally ask what I want to talk about, so I need to have a topic ready.

While Jake talks constantly about steam trains, his mom told me that some people with autism do not talk at all. Jake said they are "non-verbal." Jake is certainly not non-verbal. I wouldn't really want him to be. His mom said, although he talks a lot now, he started talking very late. Even when he was three, his mom couldn't understand a word he said.

I wanted to know how someone who was non-verbal could let their mom or their teacher know what they wanted.

Jake said that some use sign language. He told me that other people use specially designed cards with pictures and words on them. He called them PECS cards. I think Jake has a special word for everything.

Jake loves playing with words and making puns. He has to be careful though because we have another student in the class with autism and she takes everything literally.

One day the teacher said, "It's time to roll up our sleeves and get to work." She rolled up her sleeves. Everyone laughed and she walked out of the classroom. Jake just can't understand why she takes things literally.

I think not really understanding others is a part of his autism. I felt bad that we all laughed, I don't think that was very kind. Do you?

I can always tell when Jake is really stressed or really excited because he starts stimming. A stim is any behaviour that is repeated over and over again. I never used to know what stimming was, but I saw Jake do it all the time, so I asked him. Jake stims by spinning round and round on the spot, or by rocking back and forth.

Jake's dad used to try to stop Jake from stimming because he was worried that if Jake continued to spin other children would make fun of him. However, our teacher has explained to us that stimming is important because it is how autistic children are able to cope with their fear, anxiety or excitement and there is nothing wrong with stimming. She pointed out that a lot of us have repetitive actions, such as clicking a pen or twirling our hair. I asked Jake why he spins. He told me that it's comforting and he likes it. I went to the supermarket the other day, and a boy there was jumping up and down. I was exhausted just watching him. I was glad that I had Jake as a friend, as it meant that I didn't see this as odd.

Jake is the tidiest person I know. Everything has to be neat and tidy. His mom said when he was little, he used to line all his cars up in a line. Everything has to be in order and everything has to have a place.

Another thing about Jake is that he's not good at making eye contact. Sounds like it's not a big deal, but it used to really annoy me. Sometimes he even walks away when I'm talking to him. However, I have learned that Jake is not being rude and he really doesn't mean to hurt my feelings.

Jake doesn't have many friends, which is normal for autistic people. However, I have come to really appreciate how he is always honest and will never do something just to impress others, like so many of my other friends do.

It's odd, because while I know he's autistic, I tend to forget and just think of him as Jake. I just don't see him as different anymore. Well, he is different, just as I'm different from my sister, and my other friends. However, all of my friends have different interests and different ways of thinking about things.

I asked Jake, what do autistic people do
when they become adults? Jake laughed,
and said that they do the same as everyone
else. Autistic people can go to university,
get married, get a job and buy a house. I
guess, autism doesn't really make people
that different after all. I hope I'm still
Jake's friend so I can find out what he
becomes. I'm sure it will be amazing.